THE HABITUAL VISION OF EXCELLENCE

A Tribute to St. John's College and Our Tutors

On the Occasion of the 50th Reunion of the

St. John's College Class of 1961

September 23, 2011

The Tutors Honored

Eva Brann

Sam Kutler

Luke Harvey Poe, Jr.

Tom Simpson

Tom Slakey

Curtis Wilson

Malcolm Wyatt

NOTE ON THE COVER

The title given to this volume, *The Habitual Vision of Excellence*, is the title of a brochure that members of the St. John's College Class of 1961 were given as prospective students to introduce them to the College.

The background image on the cover is of McDowell Hall, the central and oldest classroom building on the College's Annapolis campus.

50th Reunion Ad Hoc Committee

Nana Dealy, Chair

Michael Ham

Marcia Goldberg Mathog

Mary Lou Ryce

Harrison Sheppard

* * * * * * * * * * * * * * * * * *

Published by:

Harrison Sheppard

Law & Conflict Resolution

191 Frederick St., No. 23

San Francisco, CA 94117

http://voicesoflife.com

http://whatsrightwithlawyers.com

hjslaw@jps.net

TABLE OF CONTENTS

i

INTRODUCTION

This booklet pays tribute to St. John's College and its tutors on the occasion of the 50th Reunion of the St. John's College Class of 1961. It is a felicitous fact that there remain a good number of tutors who were at the College when the Members of the Class of 1961 were students who are able to receive this little volume in person.

Since the heart of the St. John's College curriculum is its assigned readings of the gems of Western Literature and conversation about what they say, it is fitting that the form of these tributes mixes quotations from such great works with the personal testimonies of twenty-four Members of the Class of 1961, signifying how their experiences of the College and its tutors positively affected their lives. An outside reader of the book would obtain some idea of the College curriculum from the quotations chosen. These include brief excerpts from the writings of Heraclitus, Plato, Euclid, Chaucer, Galileo, Shakespeare, Goethe, Keats, James Clerk Maxwell, Einstein, and Camus. They also include direct references to the writings of Homer, Herodotus, Euripides, Aristotle, the Old and New Testaments, Epictetus, Plutarch, St. Augustine, Thomas Aquinas, Dante, Montaigne, Francis Bacon, Leibniz, Immanuel Kant, David Hume, John-Jacques Rousseau, William Harvey, James Madison, Jane Austen, Emily Bronte, Dostoevsky, Alexis deTocqueville, and Sigmund Freud.

What may be most striking about the use of these quotations is how they resonate through what is declared in the personal testimonies, reflecting the depth, breadth, and height of the influence of the College upon Members of the Class of 1961, viewed from the perspective of half a century of living experience after leaving the College. It is, of course, the highest tribute to St. John's College and its tutors that the liberal education they provided has proven, as demonstrated by the testimony of its former students, to remain vital—and more than merely "relevant"—to the lives they have led outside the College. These testimonies are our way of saying "Thank You" to St. John's tutors and the College for making a rich and enduring contribution to our lives.

Harrison Sheppard

San Francisco

The Tributes

On A Community of Learning

From Eyvind Ronquist

"And gladly would he learn and gladly teach."

Geoffrey Chaucer, General Prologue, *Canterbury Tales* (Describing the Oxford Cleric)

A Question That Stays With Us

From George Kell

ἔχεις μοι ειπειν ἀρα διδακτὸν η αρετή; ἢ ου διδακτὸν αλλα σκητόν;

Plato, *Meno*

On A Gift of Liberal Education
From Sarah Robinson Mara

I am a more confident person in my private and professional life because of St. John's.

On The Soul, Old and Young

From Linda McConnell

"Only connect! That was the whole of her sermon. Only connect the prose and the passion, and both will be exalted, and human love will be seen at its height. Live in fragments no longer. Only connect, and the beast and the monk, robbed of the isolation that is life to either, will die."

E.M. Forster, *Howard's End*

"I was so much older then. I'm younger than that now." **R.A. Zimmerman**

On Exhilarating Tutors and Classmates
From Linda Ferguson Dyke

When I think back to my years at St. John's, I particularly remember my freshman year, and how exhilarating it all was. Scott Abbott, Duncan McDonald, William Darkey, are some of the people who inspired those feelings. Later, Victor Zuckerkandl, Simon Kaplan, Michael Ossorgin introduced me to worlds musical and biblical. And how great to find friends among fellow students who also enjoyed reading and thinking. I am looking forward to seeing some of them again!

On the Pursuit of Knowledge

From Peg Brown Llewellyn-Jones

St. John's gave me "the means of gradually increasing my knowledge and good sense to the highest possible point which the mediocrity of my talents and the brief duration of my life can permit me to reach.....I have always had an excessive desire to learn to distinguish the true from the false, in order to see clearly in my actions and to walk with confidence in my life."

Descartes: *Discourse on the Method of Rightly Conducting the Reason*

On Confessed Ignorance

From Ken Butler

Some years back a good friend of mine who teaches English told me that he had talked about a line from one of my poems: "I don't know what I see/ When I see love." "Here's a line," he said, "that talks about seeing that doesn't use an image." I connect that line with the Socratic line, "I know only that I know nothing." I think that St. John's, with its ardors and bafflements, made me feel that it was possible to see that I didn't know, and that not-knowing was somehow sustaining, we are so frail.

On St. John's Subtle Influences
From Nancy Hubbard O'Connell

Thank you St. John's for such an important grounding early in life. Although my time at St. John's was very short, it has had a lifelong impact on my thinking (not on a conscious level, but rather in the way I approach problems, ideas, and important decisions). This is not always the most comfortable way to live, but it does result in a clearer understanding of one's choices and beliefs. There are many ideas and thoughts from our reading and classwork that come to mind frequently, but in these days of political turmoil nothing springs to mind more often than Plato's Philosopher King. Badly needed!

On Skepticism & True Learning

From Richard Freis

"Do not believe in anything simply because you have heard it. Do not believe in anything simply because it is spoken and rumored by many. Do not believe in anything simply because it is found written in your religious books. Do not believe in anything merely on the authority of your teachers and elders. Do not believe in traditions because they have been handed down for many generations. But after observation and analysis, when you find that anything agrees with reason and is conducive to the good and benefit of one and all, then accept it and live up to it."

The Buddha

"You cannot teach people anything, you can only help them find it within themselves."

Galileo Galilei

A Musical Education
(With Apologies to the Great Books)

From Nancy Clark Adler

Without question my experience at St. John's altered my life profoundly and I am thankful for it, but my memories are very dim. The most vivid ones are of first semester, freshman year and they involve music. Why do I remember what I remember best? I have no idea.

Mr. Ossorgin's music tutorial was delightful. Chorus with Mr. Zuckerkandl was a fantastic way to end the week if you liked to sing. The Friday night Concerts and the Seminar discussions on great musical works were very important to me. Mostly, however, I remember the jazz listening sessions on Friday and Saturday nights in Pinkney common room. What an education that was for me, listening to the music and the comments that followed. Such pleasant memories. Go figure.

On Mentorship in Learning

From Nana May Dealy

In the quote below, the young man, implicitly Camus himself, has had an excellent education and some caring and wise mentors prior to his association with the person he is addressing. I submit this paean with a similar degree of hyperbole to express continuing gratitude to my tutors at St. John's:

"...[W]hen I was very young, very foolish...you paid attention to me and, without seeming to, you opened for me the door to everything I love in the world.. . . .Even the most gifted person needs someone to initiate him. The one that life puts in your path one day, that person must be loved and respected forever, even if he's not responsible. That is my faith."

Albert Camus, *Le Premier Homme: The First Man*

On the Skills Acquired in Learning

From Michael Ham

When I was a student at St. John's, the program changed me in ways that I began to understand better when I became, for a time, Director of Admissions and had to explain the program—its goals, means, and methods—to prospective students. (I learned from that, and now I regularly try to explain the things I am working to understand: as we learned at St. John's, good questions lead to greater understanding, and interactive explanation is a rich source of good questions.)

We gain skills through their exercise. In the St. John's program we exercised the skills of reading, studying, questioning, listening, speaking, teaching (demonstrating math theorems, for example), translating, writing, and performing experiments. Through active exercise we acquired, practiced, and improved our skills in the liberal arts.

The works we studied required those skills—indeed, they required more skill than we had, but that was what drove the learning: our skills improved the harder they were worked, and those books demand much from us, then and now. And it is that demand that makes them so enormously rewarding.

Those demands would have been overwhelming without the guidance we got from our tutors and the help of our fellow students. Sometimes someone would help us by explaining something to us, sometimes the help would be in listening to (and questioning) our own explanations.

We were immersed in a sea of learning and change and built there a foundation for our later life and learning.

12

On the Questions Within

From Mary Lou Ryce

When I arrived at St. John's in September of 1957, I was probably one of the most naïve freshmen to enter those halls. I could have come straight from *The Little House on the Prairie*. Looking back, it is clear that our tutors used a very gentle pen on my *tabula rasa*.

How careful they were to write only questions – never answers – questions sometimes designed with subtle humor, or not so subtle humor, to reveal the world outside of the *Prairie*. Ford K. Brown seemed especially adept at challenging naively held ideas. I recall a story he told in our sophomore language tutorial about a community seminar he had taught in Baltimore. One of the participants always began any comment with, "The consensus of my opinion is..." Mr. Brown would often (it seemed) turn to me after presenting a thorny question and ask, "And, what is the consensus of your opinion, Miss Ryce?"

I have thought about that question over the years – not just the humor – but the underlying meaning: Perhaps others feel as I do that there are many persons within me – each trying to pursue a different goal? Is it not important that we reach consensus within ourselves about how to live a good life? And, how do we bring consensus within ourselves to all of the competing obligations to society, family, self? Do we not sometimes need to stand alone as "a consensus of one" in choosing to do the right thing? With the indelible ink of the Great Books, our St. John's tutors wrote many questions to challenge the naïve children who came to them in 1957; then they passed the pens to us. I am grateful.

An Anecdote of Teaching at the College

From Cynthia Bledsoe Daley

An indelible lesson I took from St. John's occurred during my first oral exam. Uncertain about how it would go, I questioned others as they emerged from theirs. Most said it was begun about like a seminar, with a tutor asking a question about one of the books we had read. I grew more apprehensive while I paced the hall waiting to be called into the room. I mentally reviewed the readings I hoped to be asked about, and thought with dread of those that I had not given much time to. When the door did open, and I was motioned in to take a seat, I was shocked to see three unsmiling tutors wearing their black robes arrayed on one side of a seminar table. Seated opposite them, I waited for the oral to start. Ignoring me, they very quietly discussed something among themselves. Then the room grew silent. Time passed while I waited. Finally, one of the tutors very kindly asked, "Miss Bledsoe, what would you like to talk about?" My mind went completely blank, and I heard my own voice saying, "Plato's Republic." That was the one reading that I had not really read carefully, the very one I had most dreaded being asked about! For the next painful hour I humiliated myself with my own ignorance. They gently asked questions that I stupidly answered, revealing how little I had understood. Finally it was over. I knew that I had failed something really important. I waited for the penalty. But I found out that I had passed with a grade of "B". I went to the tutor I was least intimidated by, and asked how that was possible. He smiled, and said, "We thought you learned a lot in that hour." For 50 years I have carried that memory. They were so very kind to an unfinished seventeen year old scholar.

The Joy of St. John's Earthquakes

From Victor Schwartz

I did not so much "go" to St. John's as I was "sent" by *The Fates*. I had never heard of it. From the sky the College catalog fell into my lap. I was amazed at the power of the curriculum, of the value of such an education—its utilitarian value!! (Mr. Kaplan must be writhing in his grave.) Indeed, after St. John's, law school was a breeze. And I'm convinced that Justice Marshall studied Euclid. His opinions are written like Euclidean propositions. But as a student at the College the utilitarian value lost its "value." It was not even a consideration.

I learned much at the College and believe anyone who ever attended for at least one semester learns much. Most likely more than he or she realizes. Even if it's by osmosis. The air is suffused with learning, reflection, and self-reflection. Every good liberal arts college rattles the minds and souls of its students. St. John's did not simply rattle; it created earthquakes—at least one for me.

Our education was not simply about Harvey and Hume, Leibniz and Lincoln, Euclid and Einstein. It was as much about life and death, God and the devil. No one attends the College and leaves "unexamined". *The unexamined life not worth living...*(What does it mean " not worth living"? Let's have a seminar.)

At the end of the junior year, Mr. Darkey recommended that I not return. Dean Wilson saved me. Saved me to return and study electromagnetism. It was magic. Unfortunately, I don't remember much of what I learned in the physics lab. What I do remember, however, as clearly as if it were this morning, was Mr. Simpson's joy and delight in tutoring that class, like a happy child playing with his toys. Apparently the appreciation of that joy had a greater impact on my life than the science. To me it was more important. The enthusiasm and joy, not only of Mr. Simpson, but of Mr. Allanbrook, Mr. Zuckerkandl, and all the integrity, dedication, and kindness of Mr. Kaplan, Mr. Ossorgin, Mr. Wilson, and *all the others* had a tremendous impact.

The greatest testimonial to the College and my tutors is that I would have loved to spend my life being a tutor there.

15

Learning Statement

From Marilyn Brinsfield Christie

Over the past weeks, I have been listening to students of Cognitive Behavioural Therapy offer to their tutors and peers a summary of their significant learning, both individual and professional, over the past academic year. These statements are always interesting and often moving as adult learners describe the challenges of being students, sometimes for the first time, at this intellectual and personally demanding level.

Like these students, entering St John's was for me crossing the portal of an expanding universe. I experienced the interaction with the learning environment and the encounter with my classmates at once terrifying, exciting and exhilarating. It was an experience for which at times I felt totally unprepared. It was also one which left me immeasurably enriched.

What I am offering here is the realization of the significance of my learning experience at St. John's, as it has become manifest in my life over the past 50 years.

I often find that I don't know what I think until someone asks the question. A good question was asked at my entrance interview by the Principal of Craigie College of Education. "At St. John's College, Mrs. Christie, what did they teach you to do?" "They taught me to think".

Another question was "Would you like to develop a Diploma in Counseling?" "Of course I would."

I remember my colleague saying "Let's write the kind of course we would like to attend." I immediately recalled my experience at St. John's and it was that experience which informed the *ethos,* structure and content of the course we wrote.

Hundreds of students have now graduated from this course and when they offer their "learning statements" the recurring theme has been "This has been the best learning experience of my life." That is true of my experience at St John's

As a result of these experiences I have become a Cognitive Behavioural Psychotherapist. This is an appropriate destination for a St. Johnnie, as the therapeutic tool central to CBT is Socratic Questioning.

St. John's is to me: Reading, Thinking, Questioning, Discussing, and Learning. What I remember most about our tutors was the respect they showed to us, their encouragement for us to find our voices, their skill in facilitation and their ability to maintain a structure that enabled learning to flourish. I have had a lifetime in which to learn to appreciate what they taught me.

On Beauty, Truth, & Light
From Marcia Goldberg Mathog

This seminar reading at Stag's Leap led by Miss Brann opened my mind to a whole new world of possibilities:

Ode on a Grecian Urn

Thou still unravish'd bride of quietness,
Thou foster-child of silence and slow time,
Sylvan historian, who canst thus express
A flowery tale more sweetly than our rhyme:
What leaf-fring'd legend haunt about thy shape
Of deities or mortals, or of both,
In Tempe or the dales of Arcady?
What men or gods are these? What maidens loth?
What mad pursuit? What struggle to escape?
What pipes and timbrels? What wild ecstasy?

Heard melodies are sweet, but those unheard
Are sweeter: therefore, ye soft pipes, play on;
Not to the sensual ear, but, more endear'd,
Pipe to the spirit ditties of no tone:
Fair youth, beneath the trees, thou canst not leave
Thy song, nor ever can those trees be bare;
Bold lover, never, never canst thou kiss,
Though winning near the goal - yet, do not grieve;
She cannot fade, though thou hast not thy bliss,
For ever wilt thou love, and she be fair!

Ah, happy, happy boughs! that cannot shed
Your leaves, nor ever bid the spring adieu;
And, happy melodist, unwearied,

For ever piping songs for ever new;
More happy love! more happy, happy love!
For ever warm and still to be enjoy'd,
For ever panting, and for ever young;
All breathing human passion far above,
That leaves a heart high-sorrowful and cloy'd,
A burning forehead, and a parching tongue.

Who are these coming to the sacrifice?
To what green altar, O mysterious priest,
Lead'st thou that heifer lowing at the skies,
And all her silken flanks with garlands drest?
What little town by river or sea shore,
Or mountain-built with peaceful citadel,
Is emptied of this folk, this pious morn?
And, little town, thy streets for evermore
Will silent be; and not a soul to tell
Why thou art desolate, can e'er return.

O Attic shape! Fair attitude! with brede
Of marble men and maidens overwrought,
With forest branches and the trodden weed;
Thou, silent form, dost tease us out of thought
As doth eternity: Cold Pastoral!
When old age shall this generation waste,
Thou shalt remain, in midst of other woe
Than ours, a friend to man, to whom thou say'st,
"Beauty is truth, truth beauty," - that is all
Ye know on earth, and all ye need to know.

John Keats, 1819

From 40 years of pondering why we had to learn vector calculus:

Let there be light:

$$\nabla \cdot \mathbf{E} = \frac{\rho}{\varepsilon_0}$$

$$\nabla \cdot \mathbf{B} = 0$$

$$\nabla \times \mathbf{E} = -\frac{\partial \mathbf{B}}{\partial t}$$

$$\nabla \times \mathbf{B} = \mu_0 \mathbf{J} + \mu_0 \varepsilon_0 \frac{\partial \mathbf{E}}{\partial t}$$

A Treatise on Electricity and Magnetism, James Clerk Maxwell, 1873

Because one quote or another from Goethe seems to always be with me:

"...a confusion of the real with the ideal never goes unpunished."

Elective Affinities, **Johann Wolfgang von Goethe, 1809**

A Gratitude

From Peter Nabokov

My main memory of the instructors at St. Johns is how hard they worked, how much they cared and how great the sacrifice paid by their families. Of course at my age, and as a failed member of the class who was fairly immature and lacked the ability to focus on written texts for very long, I may blur my actual student years at St. Johns with those before. Having started at 16, then leaving, returning and leaving again, it is hard to recall continuity. What constancy I do remember comes from earlier on and being a son at age one, then a stepson at age nine, of two St. John's faculty members, and so my recollections are of a continuity of tall, serious, sometimes jaunty, tie-wearing and tweed-jacketed mostly men who, from the aftermath of the Second World War onward, I knew as the reigning elders of my youth. Never since, ever, have I sensed such collective devotion in a work place, such effort of time and thought and that force of what I can only call *mission* behind it all. Monday, Thursday and Friday evenings Bill Darkey ate his dinner with us at a bit of a clip, kissed my mother then took off out the back door, through yard and its rear metal fence, out onto Lafayette Street, past Earle's grocery, with myself and his complaining loyal cat Figaro joining him until the three of us reached the corner of the block – my boyhood limit those early evenings. And when he returned around ten I often would wake to hear my mother debrief him, as she would also do after the endless instruction committees when their discussions would be especially intense as I gathered serious explorations and differences of opinion had ensued over matters of importance – not over our finances or any promotion but issues of values, ideals, intellectual directions, books. And then he would be up before me, reading for seminars, translating for tutorials, figuring equations for math, listening to music with the scores on his lap – and I felt the rest of them must have been doing the same, Curtis Wilson, Simon Kaplan, Winfree Smith, all of them who always smiled kindly at me. I just remember these examples of the importance of the life of the mind as signifying that absolutely nothing was more central about being human on this earth, nor never divorced from action. And when any new tutors responded positively about being welcomed and absorbed into this surround-sound life of the mind, I remember how excited it made my stepfather and my mother, and that is how remarkable individuals like Alfred Satterthwaite and Victor Zuckerkandl loom in my memory, and of course later on with Eva Brann who captured my parents love and respect right away. My God, those tall tall men, Bill Darkey, Corky Kramer, then Tom Simpson and the rest – how profoundly they cared, how hard they read, and then read again, how much St. Johns was what they *became,* and how that love of learning became them. Divergent as they were in personalities, scholarly expertise and even, perhaps in institutional commitment, I just sensed that they shared such a passion for words, thoughts, ethics, books, art that I had and wanted no choice about sharing it too. Perhaps I'm fooling myself here, and have idealized this summarizing memory, but it has sustained me all my life - so be it.

The Perfect St. Johnnie

From Michael W. Gold

How did St. John's affect my life?

It turned my life upside down, and it did it in the first fifteen minutes of the first seminar. Like every pompous adolescent from Brooklyn in those days, I thought Sigmund Freud had the answer to everything, and I came into seminar prepared to explain to everybody that the theme of the poem was the homosexual relationship between Achilles and Patroclus. Thus I hastened to begin the education of my classmates. There followed a few simple questions—I don't remember from whom, but I like to think they were from tobacco farmers' daughters or Maryland Scholarship recipients from the backwoods of Western Maryland—kids who had not had my advantages. *And I could not answer them!* There was a little desultory discussion, and the seminar moved on.

In those ten or fifteen minutes it hit me that that is not what *The Iliad* is about at all, that Homer was about...*something else*...and I did not know what it was. Ever since, I have been trying to work my way back, to see as Homer and the ancient authors of our tradition saw, or rather, to try and figure out how we who cannot see, and cannot understand, must live.

Did it help me? It didn't make me the star of cocktail parties, like we all said it would. I had a decent career, but it took me 25 years to find the work that really suited me. When I found the work that suited me (I was a commercial real estate appraiser), I always took the thorny and unremunerative assignments that my colleagues had better sense than to mess with. I wrote the best reports in the entire history of the Commonwealth of Virginia; but no one cared: a workaday report would have done just as well. I was well respected for my work, but much of the time I made less than my plumber. Socially, I have found (as someone said) I cannot talk to those I pray with, and I cannot pray with those I talk to...except that I can't really pray, and I don't talk much either. I want to *know*, but my brain is only half up to the task. That makes me an intellectual, and I hate intellectuals. I have interesting ideas (I do!), but even those who love me know that I am often a hairsbreadth from a jerk.

One thing I learned at St. John's (to single out just one thing, but this one goes back to that very first seminar) is the fatality of anger, and related to it—a thread of steel running through the whole program—that the imagination of man's heart is evil from his youth. I love my country (both countries) but I am terribly frightened for the future. I work in my garden. I love nature; but it always intrudes upon me that nature is red in tooth and claw. I think it must be true that it is best not to have been born.

...and yet. The girl I married fell in love with me because she'd never met a mind like mine. My wife and my children sometimes smile condescendingly (I know they do), but they love me. My little grandchildren love me too, though I think I already see the beginning of condescension in the charming smile of the six-year-old.

The world stinks all the same. But I am a happy man. I went into St. John's a dumb kid from Brooklyn. I came out the perfect St. Johnnie.

On Scholarship

From John C. Kohl Jr.

Some years after graduation from St. John's College, I came across a copy of Gilbert Highet's *The Classical Tradition* (New York: Oxford University Press, 1949). It was a splendid read, and the twenty-first chapter, entitled "a Century of Scholarship," was especially striking and influential to me. I quote here a few brief excerpts:

"This belief that the study and teaching of the classical literatures ought to be purely and scientifically objective has spoilt many a teacher and many, many good pupils. It was largely responsible for the recession in public interest in the classics during the latter half of the nineteenth century. Put broadly, it has meant that classical scholars feel more obliged to extend knowledge than to disseminate it. The gap between the scholar and the public, which in the Renaissance and in the revolutionary era was bridged by a constant interflow of teaching and questioning and propaganda and imitation and translation and emulation, has now widened to a gulf.

"It is well exemplified in the paradoxical life of A. E. Housman. He was a fine poet, and a sensitive, though limited, critic of letters. But his chief work in the classics consisted of trying to establish the original text of Propertius, Juvenal, Lucan, and Manilius—that is, of removing the mistakes and unintelligibilities introduced into their poems by ignorant copyists and medieval scholars. Difficult and necessary as this is, it is ultimately a glorified form of proof-reading. And he did not care particularly for these four poets, or said he did not.... Housman did not explain in detail why anyone should choose to study Greek and Latin literature rather than the Calypso songs of Trinidad and the hymns of the Tibetan monasteries (which would also provide intricate subjects of study); but in a rapid sentence or two... he said it was a matter of personal preference. Would he have refused to admit that the writings of the Greeks and Romans are objectively and universally, more beautiful? That they are more relevant to us, who are at some removes their spiritual descendants?

25

"It is, then, the fundamental fault of modern classical scholarship that it has cultivated research more than interpretation, that it has been more interested in the acquisition than in the dissemination of knowledge, that it has denied or disdained the relevance of its work in the contemporary world, and that it has encouraged the public neglect of which it now complains. The scholar has a responsibility to society—not less, but greater, than that of the laborer and the business man. His first duty is to know the truth, and his second is to make it known. For classical scholarship is one of the main channels through which the uniquely valuable influence of the culture of Greece and Rome, still living and fertile, still incalculably stimulating, can be communicated to the modern world—the world that it has already, not once but twice and thrice and oftener, saved from the repeated attacks of materialism and barbarism."

These remarks of Highet, a professor of Latin at Columbia University in New York, were written well over sixty years ago. If anything, the gap between scholar and public which he mentions seems to me to have widened now, and the extent of scientific specialization, it seems to me, has, if anything, spread with the ensuing years from Greek and Latin studies into all areas of literature, history, philosophy, and kindred subjects and rendering by stages and degrees the college catalog into a text of irrelevancies. If we are to continue to read, write, and converse about these subjects and to benefit from their civilizing influences, then, paradoxically, scholars now bear the responsibility of preventing their subject matter from disintegrating under their noses by their own scholarly activity and from a fate far worse and more permanent than the temporary eclipses by the incursions of barbarians of the past: an implosion from within.

St. John's Influence On an Educator

From David Shapiro

Thoughts and feelings about my experience at St. John's, at least through June 11, 2011, from a student who:

took up teaching in non-public schools, in '67;

teaching and 'administration' in a new, 7-12 public school, in '76;

full time building administration in an old public high school in '87;

and full time reflection on education upon retirement starting in '09.

SJC has been an essential element in framing my work in education.

I have collected a few quotations. If not epiphanic, they represent some insight in my work as teacher, learner, leader and 'school master'. Start with Francis Bacon, *A prudent question is one half of wisdom.* (There's another one I also like from Russell Ackoff, who wrote in a more recent century that it is more helpful to get a wrong answer to the right question than to get a right answer to the wrong question.)

My first teaching job was teaching algebra. And the question was and continues to be, why do so many students find it difficult? Lucky for me, it was also Caleb Gattegno's question: How can I get pupils personally interested in numbers and their relationships? Gattegno found George Cuisenaire, and provided guidance for teaching arithmetic and algebra with Cuisenaire rods.

My second job was teaching introductory physical science and chemistry. There was a great difference between learning science in school and learning science as a technician with researchers. I struggled in school courses. As a technician, I learned the scientific method and what scientists were about. Question: What's involved in teaching science in school?

What is instruction? Robert Gagné* started with "What is learning?" in 1940 when, as an Army Air Corps training designer, he was asked to find a way to instruct non-teachers to make airplane mechanics out of farmers in 30 days instead of two years of trial and error. Military training was no different in 1940 than from my own experience in 1962. A cadre of instructors was responsible for instruction, which differed for different types of learning outcomes. There was a tacit assumption that the instructional events do not 'produce' learning, but are conditions that support a student's learning 'process'. Success or lack of it in this milieu was a problem for instructors to solve. The 'tacit assumption' in my public schools has been the opposite. The rhetoric of conflicting views on public education today reveals the differences. The question: What happens in school when a student does not learn?

My third job included teaching, supervising other teachers, and leading the math and science programs in a public school. The context was institutional and political. Public responsibilities needed publicly accepted credentials. I had to enroll in a grad program in educational administration. A new door opened, but the terrain was familiar. I opted to write a thesis in lieu of several 'courses'.

---

* *The Conditions of Learning and Theory of Instruction*, 4th ed., p. 2.

I studied a school 'culture' and school change with some basic ethnographic methods. The question: What do people want from their schools?

My fourth job, high school assistant principal, came through an ephemeral effort at an old high school to adopt the principles and practices of Ted Sizer's Coalition of Essential Schools. As a 'Johnnie', I was an exotic who had experience in such a program. The attendant (and predictably bitter) conflict within the faculty social system to remain the same: excellent example of Donald Schön's 'dynamic conservatism'. The question: what does it take a school to transform, or change anything at all?

In the fifties, Edgar Schein studied returning POWs from the Korean conflict who differed greatly in how they responded to coercion as prisoners. Schein developed his understanding of coercion as he extended it in his work with corporations on leadership and organizational change. He contended that leadership and organizational change were 'two sides of the same coin'. Does there have to be a crisis to bring about change? How about coercion?

The following quotes and sources resonate most within the framework I have developed around education, including my experience at SJC.

Perhaps the greatest idea that America has given the world is education for all. The world is entitled to know whether this idea means that everybody can be educated or simply that everyone must go to school. **--Robert M. Hutchins, 1972**

We can, whenever and wherever we choose, successfully teach all children whose schooling is of interest to us. We already know more than we need to do that. Whether or not we do it must finally depend on how we feel about the fact that we haven't so far. **--Ronald Edmonds, c. 1975**

Long before Bettelheim, Immanuel Kant had given profound support to the proposition that, in human affairs generally, "love is not enough." The more basic gift is not love but respect, respect for others as ends in themselves, as actual and potential artisans of their own learnings and doings, of their own lives; and as thus uniquely contributing, in turn, to the learnings and doings of others. **David Hawkins, c. 1974**

Too smart to study. Too cute to care. **–Anon,** from a poster given to my daughter at age 7, picturing kittens with large bows in a gift basket.

We have met the enemy and he is us. **"Pogo", Walt Kelley, Earth Day 1970**

Looking at the College After Fifty Years
From Rev. Douglas Bendall, Ph.D.

I keep on my desk at home as a constant reminder Euclid's definition of a unit. It reads:

"A unit is that according to which each of the beings is said to be one." (Bk. VII, Def. 1).

We were young then—I was just 18—when we were assigned this text, and I recall thinking that it implied a promise the College might fulfill. What is it indeed "according to which each of the beings" can be recognized as one thing and thus be counted? I wondered: Will this school teach me this? It seemed marvelous to me that there may be an answer to this question and St. John's College might be able to provide it.

I came to St. John's on a quest. My first memories as a child involved an awareness of a world at war. I still grieved over the death of a beloved uncle who gave his life in battle off Okinawa toward the end of WWII. My mind was filled with the horrendous photos of Holocaust victims that Life Magazine was publishing. These articles in Life were my first encounter with serious reading matter. They were disturbing; and their subject was all too real. How, I wondered, could human beings be so cruel to others? In hope of finding an answer to this question, I gave up my original plan to study civil engineering at Johns Hopkins University and then build dams in poor countries to seek answers to questions about the good and the evil that life presents. How, I thought, can we seek to solve problems in poorer countries, when we have so many unresolved problems of our own?

Fifty years later, the questions I brought to St. John's are still alive in me, as they are perhaps in the reader. The following is (roughly) the way I frame them now.

31

The answer to the question I posed about Euclid's monads was explored in depth by Leibniz in his *Monadology*. We read the texts; but much of what they contained escaped us, perhaps because of our inexperience. Like so much of what is present in my mind, my own thinking originated from and was shaped by the books we read and the life of the College as a whole. Here is what happened to me. I used to watch my fellow students in addition to reading the books. With time, I came to see there was a good fit between the thoughts we expressed in seminar and the way we walked and otherwise expressed our being. Difficult conversations, sometimes overheard in the coffee shop, eventually led me to see that our humanity cannot be taken for granted. It was in the community, living among and with my fellow students, that I first found the answer to the burning question I brought with me to the College. It is this: Our humanity is not given by nature; it is an achievement. The Holocaust occurred because human beings had forgotten that becoming fully human is an art that requires our best efforts. Somehow we had been lulled into the belief that our humanity is something given by nature, a simple datum.

In our Junior year, I decided to work on becoming fully human. It was this that led me eventually into theology, ministry in the Episcopal Church, and fourteen years ago, the founding of The Newark School of Theology, in which theology is taught as a liberal art. Our work in New Jersey is inspired by the motto of our College; namely, "I make free adults out of children by means of books and a balance." It is also guided by a remarkable sight I saw at the College so many years ago. I walked into a seminar room alone one morning after Jacob Klein had lectured on the meaning of the Divided Line in the *Republic*. His diagram was still on the board. As I studied it, I realized that, for Mr. Klein, Plato's insights express a dimension that is properly termed theological. The Divided Line points towards God. I never forgot what Mr. Klein was showing us. After all these years, I now realize that Mr. Klein and the other refugees from war-torn Europe, who contributed so much to the making of the College in its present form, were adults who lived through the dramatic events I read about in *Life Magazine* when I was a child. They had thought deeply about the meaning of human life and knew through personal experience that our humanity can indeed be lost; that to achieve it requires a liberal arts education of the type they, the founders of the New Program, and other members of the faculty created in Annapolis. Jacob, the brilliant scholar and Russian Jew who converted to Christianity—even as he remained thoroughly Jewish— also saw the connection between the study of the liberal arts and faith in God. The unity of the beings is derived from the unity of God, who is the author of all beings.

"Wisdom is one thing: To know the *logos* by which all things are steered through all things." **Heraclitus**

The first commandment is this: "Hear, O Israel: The Lord our God is the only Lord. Love your God with all your heart, with all your soul, with all your mind, and with all your strength. The second is this: Love your neighbor as yourself. There is no other commandment greater than these." *Mark* **12:29-31;** cited in *The Book of Common Prayer*, **p. 351.**

On Being Inspired By the College & Tutors

From Harrison Sheppard

This is a love letter to St. John's College and to those of its tutors with whom I have had the privilege to converse and learn; for I boast myself to be among the most devoted of the College's many lovers.

I fell in love with the College as a prospective student, and my immediate passion for it was heated by a flame that propelled me to visit it twice as a high school senior, staying a full two weeks the second time, so that, on my entering the College as a freshman, Albert, the College watchman, thought I was a returning classman. My passion for the College even as a prospective student was evident to James M. Tolbert, Director of Admissions at the time, who gave me the student assistance job as Prospective Student Guide, an occupation that was a delightful labor of love, and one I continued through my sophomore year.

My freshman year seemed an entrance to Paradise, with the gate opened by Jacob Klein's first Friday night (Dean's) lecture. His subject was the Delphic Oracle's admonition "Know Thyself." The lecture had to be given in the gymnasium that night --the Great Hall was then under some repair—and I left the gymnasium a transformed boy, hypnotized (or perhaps, more aptly said, awakened) by what Jascha had to say about the philosophic enterprise. My four-year stay in Paradise was, as every St. John's student will probably attest, interrupted by periods of Purgatorial travails and Hellish self-doubt but, nevertheless, on the day of my graduation, I returned to my dormitory room to collect my trunk and sat on it, sobbing, before I could collect myself enough to leave the campus.

My devotion to the College has persisted throughout my years as an alumnus, leading me to be among the founders of the San Francisco Chapter of the St. John's College Alumni Association, a Member of the Alumni Board, and a Member of the College's Board of Visitors and Governors—the latter an honor I cherish as much as any other in my life, except one. The superlative honor was being given the privilege of delivering a Friday night lecture at the Santa Fe campus of the College on November 5, 2004. (The lecture, titled "The Hazardous Future of Democracy in America: Tocqueville and Lawyers in America," was adapted and appropriately published as a tribute to Eva Brann in *The Envisioned Life: Essays in Honor of Eva Brann*, Paul Dry Books, Philadelphia, 2007).*

The preceding College biography is offered as testimony to my love of it. As my life's partner, Joy, has frequently reminded me in gauging the truth of a matter: "Don't listen to what people say; look at what they do." On the other hand, sometimes words are deeds, and this love letter would not be fully truthful if it did not include some confessions of the kinds authorized by St. Augustine, Michel Montaigne, and Jean-Jacques Rousseau.

To begin with, my love has, in some respects, been a permanent *intoxication*. I met Socrates and Plato when I was only 16 years old, through an ecstatic reading of the *Apology*; but ancient Greek philosophy took me completely within its power when I was reintroduced to it by Jacob Klein and Eva Brann, and I have never since been able to escape its embrace. Socrates, Plato, and other culprits of intellectual and spiritual seduction who are among the greatest teachers at St. John's—including, most notably for me, Dante—have permeated my spiritual bones to their marrow.

*If I am permitted the license to consider my Prospective Student job as a part of the St. John's College Administration, and my Friday night lecture as participation in College instruction, it gives me immeasurable pleasure to think that, at one time or another, I have participated in every major aspect of the life of the College—which includes being the Founding Editor of the first College publication collecting writings by students, tutors, alumni, and Members of the College Administration and Board, *The St. John's College Bulletin*, founded in 1960 and continuing through 1962.

Being inhabited by the teachings of genius can operate like a toxin in the sublunar sphere. The "Habitual Vision of Excellence" promoted by the College can seem to be an exemplar of the truth of the maxim "The best is often enemy to the good;" for that vision has often led me to give less attention than I might otherwise have given to the spheres of my ordinary habitations through the years. Consequently, I must confess to falling far short in my life from the noble images of thought and action to which the College curriculum repeatedly exposed us. (Plutarch was, fittingly, among my favorites.) The devil is, of course, in the details, but I am loth to burden this love letter with them. Instead, now that I am in my eighth decade of life, I feel prepared to state some conclusions about the effects of the habitual vision of excellence that mesmerized me at St. John's College.

My main conclusion is that of an undeterred lover, and it might be considered a highly *romantic* one. It proceeds from the teachings of the heart far more than from logical propositions of mind. It is, moreover, akin to Dostoevsky's saying that "If Christ was not the Truth, I would still prefer Christ to the Truth." It was, without doubt, naïve and romantic of me—and not a little imprudent—to suppose that my life could unfold and elevate itself to a stature commensurate with the high dignity and status of "the Greats" (as Oxford and Cambridge termed them). My intoxication with the almost magical elixirs of the College experience has led to many failures. Perhaps prime among the longer-term failures has been a stubborn inability to count money important enough for me to absolutely ensure my family's financial security for the remaining years of my life. Indeed, I have been accused of leading my life *as if* I were very wealthy. St. John's gave me the gift and the burden of believing that *I am in fact* very wealthy, as I still believe I am. For among my dearest friends remain Homer, Socrates, Plato, and Euclid; Epictetus and Plutarch; the authors of *Ecclesiastes* and the *Psalms*; Thomas Aquinas, Dante, and Dostoevsky; James Madison and Abraham

36

Lincoln. Though my adoration of these heroes and friends has not spurred me to acquire great material wealth, it has enabled me, as a practicing lawyer for over 40 years, to sleep restfully on the soft pillow of an easy conscience. I temper this boast, however, with Solon's wisdom as reported by Herodotus concerning how a man's happiness should be judged, and Shakespeare's solace that "It sufficeth that the day will end, and then the end is known" (Brutus, in *Julius Caesar*).

I conclude this love letter to the College with a prose poem to the integrity of the College's tutors, stated metaphorically in Albert Einstein's tribute to Max Planck in **Principles of Research** **(1918)** for the character of his pursuit of the *scientific* (as opposed to the moral) enterprise:

"In the temple of science there are many mansions, and various indeed are they that dwell therein and the motives that have led them thither. Many take to science out of a joyful sense of superior intellectual power; science is their own special sport to which they look for vivid experience and the satisfaction of ambition; many others are to be found in the temple who have offered the products of their brains on this altar for purely utilitarian purposes. Were an angel of the Lord to come and drive all the people belonging to these two categories out of the temple, it would be noticeably emptier, but there would still be some, of both present and past time, left inside...Our Planck is one of them, and that is why we love him...There he sits, our beloved Planck, and smiles inside himself at my childish playing-about with the lantern of Diogenes. Our affection for him needs no threadbare explanation..."

Influences of St. John's

From Paul Rosenberg, M.D.

I had my first introduction to Greek tragedy sitting in the 4th century B.C. limestone amphitheatre at Epidaurus on the Peloponnese Peninsula watching a performance of Euripides' *Medea*. I couldn't understand the words, but the power of the play with the Greek chorus singing with the ominous mood of the play was overwhelming. It was the early summer of 1957 and I was spending six months in Europe, riding a bicycle from Paris to Rome, then travelling by boat to Piraeus through the Corinth Canal. I had been to the Acropolis and seen The Lion Gate at Mycenae. Later, I spent time in the Greek islands on my way to Turkey. I knew I would be attending St. John's in the fall and relished this wonderful introduction during the time I spent in Greece. From Turkey I intended to go through Syria and sneak across the border into Israel. Well, I was just 17 and a bit naïve. When I was taken off the train after crossing from Turkey into Syria at gun point, I realized I had definitely made a mistake. Fortunately, I was released and was able to return to Turkey. I made it to Israel by boat from Istanbul. On the way, the Israeli passengers were so eager to hear Rock and Roll that I had to sing "Rock Around The Clock" repeatedly.

Little did I know what a profound and delightful experience St. John's would be for me. My trip to Greece made the first year an intense and exciting experience for me as we were exposed to the splendor of Greek philosophy and culture made all the more vivid by my recent travels there. The gentleness of the tutors like Jacob Klein, Eva Brann, Winfree Smith, and Douglas Allanbrook, who challenged and guided us as we explored Western thought made learning a true delight. I felt fortunate to have so many classmates who contributed so much to the seminar discussions. I remember as a senior

38

walking back from the boat house one sunny afternoon in early spring and suddenly realizing this was my last year and thinking with real sadness: "This can't be over."

From St. John's, I went to Stanford Medical School in a five year program that allowed the students to work in research labs half time during the first three pre-clinical years. I worked in a genetics lab where each month a student had to present a research topic to the others in the lab. After one of my presentations, the professor in charge of the lab took me aside and said, "We have students from Harvard and Yale in this lab, but your presentations are by far the best. You come from this little school hardly anyone has ever heard of. How did you learn to give such excellent seminars?" I hadn't realized how positively he felt about my efforts. I responded that it was all because of my experience at St. John's where we had to present our ideas in seminars regularly.

The experience of participating in the seminars with the perspicacious students and faculty of St. John's helped me enormously through the years. Following medical school, I moved to Los Angeles and helped to found the Los Angeles Free Clinic. Then I started training in a psychiatric residency. During one vacation early in my second year, I revisited Greece, traveled through Iran to visit the ruins of Xerxes' palace of Persepolis, went to Afghanistan where I traveled overland through the Khyber Pass into Pakistan and on to India where I stopped to spend time on a Kashmiri houseboat on Lake Dal near Srinagar in northwest India. What I had learned about thinking through problems at St. John's served me well in Kashmir when the owners of the houseboat, who had learned I was a doctor, asked me to help their brother who was catatonic and dying because he refused to eat.

They took me to the home of their clan, a little fishing village of five or six houses on an island in Lake Dal. They carried their moribund brother out of one house and propped

39

him up against a wall. I suddenly looked around at this isolated but scenic location at the foot of the Himalayas and began to have a panic attack. How was I to help this dying man? Fortunately, I got focused and controlled my anxiety by remembering that doctors need to first take a history to find out what could be wrong. I asked what had happened to their brother. "Nothing," they said; "one day he stopped talking and then stopped eating." They took him to the psychiatric hospital where he was given injections which didn't help and sent him home to die. So, here he was in front of me, a thin, motionless and seemingly unresponsive brother in this poor village where the dark haired children had blonde bands in their long hair which I knew indicated that they suffered from a form of Kwashiorkor, an intermittent protein deficiency in their diet causing their hair to lose pigment.

To better understand my patient, I asked, in front of the assembled village sitting silently in a large circle around us, how was this brother different from his other brothers? The reply was that he was more religious than the other brothers and had never married. I understood this to suggest that he had a more fragile personality, unable to form a relationship with a woman, and that he most likely used his more rigorous religious observance to stabilize himself psychologically. But what could have traumatized him causing him to withdraw and become catatonic?

I asked if anything happened in the village in the months prior to his becoming sick. "Nothing," they said. I persisted and asked if anything happened to anyone in those months? They finally said that some men from another clan had attacked his older brother but he wouldn't let the other brothers retaliate fearing a blood feud in which someone would be killed. It was a month or two later that their religious brother's sickness had begun.

40

At first I thought that perhaps the sick brother had resentments toward his older brother about which he felt guilty when the other clan showed their aggression against his brother. So, through my translator, I asked the sick brother if he had anger in his heart towards his older brother, like the men who attacked his older brother. With a single, almost imperceptible movement, the catatonic brother shook his head indicating, "No."

Thinking back to the importance of honor to the Greeks, I realized what might be wrong. I asked could it be that when his older brother wouldn't let him fight for him, he felt dishonored; that his older brother didn't love him. There was a long pause. Then, with a more visible nod, he indicated he agreed with what I had suggested. The eldest brother, who had sat quietly during these proceedings, leaped up and embraced his limp younger brother yelling, "Of course I love you. I just didn't want anyone to get killed." Weakly, his younger brother, who had for months been silent, suddenly started to talk: "I thought I did something wrong, that you didn't love me when you wouldn't let me fight for you." They cried in each other's arms as tears came to many eyes including my own. The younger brother soon began eating again and recovered. To thank me, the village brought a 20 course "Persian feast" to my boat which I knew they could ill afford. I dared not refuse lest I dishonor them. I ate sparingly knowing the village would make good use of the food. I have always felt that more than my limited psychiatric training at the time, it was St. John's training to think problems through that allowed me to save that man's life.

I have practiced psychiatry in Los Angeles since completing my residency. Eleven years ago, I became Medical Director of eGetgoing, a dot com company dealing with addiction treatment. My team developed the first Internet-based group therapy program. The programs were far more successful than we could have imagined. Some of our live online groups had members participating from Africa, Europe, Russia and all over the U.S. We also developed addiction risk assessment evaluations for adolescents that students took online. The results could be used by their high school counselors to identify which of their students were at risk of addiction. We developed online adolescent treatment programs as well. After leaving eGetgoing, I became involved in a Canadian Internet company that provides services to impaired physicians and other groups. We are currently working on a project to extend treatment services to underserved native populations in Canada to treat substance abuse. These are exciting opportunities to use the Internet and the things I have learned to help others.

About three years ago, I noticed I was getting short of breath and becoming easily fatigued after mild exertion. At first I was diagnosed and treated for asthma, but when that didn't help, I referred myself to an outstanding pulmonologist at UCLA. He determined that I had a far more serious illness called pulmonary fibrosis, a condition in which the lung loses its elasticity and oxygen transfer is impaired. Initially, I was thought to have 2-5 years to live. With further study it was determined that I am fortunate to have a form of pulmonary fibrosis where the further loss of lung function is preventable. I have been able to minimize my limitations by losing weight and carefully watching my diet. My pulmonary function has stabilized, so further impairment may not occur. Since my lung function is limited, I continue to fatigue easily which restricts my activities. I am mostly retired, only seeing a few patients a week. My loving wife, Robin, who has been my collaborator in a treatment center I developed and in these Internet projects, is very supportive and takes good care of me. My illness prevents me from attending our 50th reunion, but my heart and greetings go out to all of you. I wish I could attend as I would like to see you all again and learn about the paths in life that you have taken and hear your perspectives on the unique and most valuable educational experience that we all shared.

ACKNOWLEDGMENTS

We express our thanks to each Member of the St. John's College Class of 1961 whose contributions are the substance of *The Habitual Vision of Excellence.* Special thanks are due to Nana Dealy, Chairman of the 50th Reunion Committee, for her extraordinary efforts soliciting timely contributions for the book and for her continuous astute editorial assistance reviewing manuscript drafts. Special thanks are likewise due to Michael Ham for his ongoing assistance and advice on formatting the draft manuscript for publication, and to his wife, Jennifer Vine, for her artful and diligent work preparing the front and back covers and managing text graphics. We express appreciation to Jo Ann Mattson in the College Alumni Office for providing alumni contact information and the back cover text. I am also grateful to my assistant, Julian Burman, for producing pre-publication mock-ups of the book to assist in its formatting. Our profound gratitude is expressed to Ariel Winnick of the St. John's College Class of 2011 for his indispensable contribution preparing the draft manuscript for the printer and its publication in proper format. *The Habitual Vision of Excellence* would not, of course, have been possible but for the inspiration the tutors of St. John's College gave the Members of the Class of 1961 to produce it.

Harrison Sheppard, Editor

APPENDIX

IN MEMORIAM

In Memory of Deceased Members of the Class of 1961:

Eric Anderson Arnold, Jr.
Armin Julius Bendiner
Leo Joseph Atkinson Craig
George DcPue, III
Peter deRaat
Nicolas Horlin Ekstrom
Bruce Theodore Faatz
Lynn Winterdale Franklin
Michael Waldo Hernandez Heady
Carole Luise Reuther Hill
Judith Anita Morganstern Licht
Ellen Martina Luff
Kenneth Harlan Marcus
Stephen D. Morrow
Pamela Van Dyck Parker Pattie
Walter Francis Pope
Theodore Barnes Stinchecum
Richard Woody West
Martha Goldstein Wyatt
William George Yovankin

IN MEMORY OF TED STINCHECUM

by Eva Brann

It was sad to hear of Ted's death. There is always a certain sense of indignation when a teacher hears of a student's dying. – It seems unnatural, since having been someone's teacher seems to carry with it a permanent relation of being the elder, of being slated to go first. It's against nature for the young to precede in death.

And Ted was young, permanently young to me. We came to St. John's College together in 1957, he as a freshman student, I as a freshman tutor. This class of 1961, which will be celebrating its fiftieth anniversary at Homecoming this fall—almost unthinkably without Ted—was, small as it was, full of memorable members. Even then Ted Stinchecum (as we know him; later he changed his name as members of his profession do) – was distinguished within this distinctive lot. He was sophisticated and demandingly particular where the rest of us, myself included, were still callow and rambunctious. It was his nature – I can imagine him as a toddler anxiously demanding perfection.

Even as a youth he was already a man of the stage. The plays he put on for us were usually exquisite in stage design and costuming. For the latter he had found the perfect collaborator in Amanda Mayer. He did his own scripts – not always intelligible to me, but always beautiful.

Theatre was within him personally as well. When he was miserable, which was often, he projected all the world's woes. When life had met his large demands, he glowed.

He had authority in our small community; he had the stuff of a benevolent tyrant that a director needs, and he made fine things happen.

I saw him rarely in the ensuing half century. A heart-warming occasion was one of those decadal anniversary parties our classes celebrate (I forget which), when he delivered a talk in my honor that combined elegance with accuracy – the way we like to hear ourselves to be spoken of. I wish I had it; he promised to turn it in to me, but he didn't –and I recalled that it was always hard to get a paper out of him.

Now that I've had to talk for him, I've done it with half the elegance but with equal warmth of feeling. Let me add that I'm very sorry never to have got to know his life's companion, Jerry. My thoughts are with him and with an ever-young, totally inimitable Ted.

For Ted & The Other Members of the Class of 1961 Who Are No Longer with Us

Thou Impatient Lover, Death

Deaf to entreaties

When you choose to take someone else's love,

Always jealous to embrace

The best beloved of others,

Ever declaring

Your wait has been too long

And never minding the grief

Of those you leave behind,

Knowing you will have them too,

Though never soon enough.

But we will outwit you,

Keeping our loves alive in spirit

With a warmth you will never know

In the cold depth of your shadowy horizons.

And when you come for us

In your skinless, boney self,

We will also triumph

Knowing we were flesh and blood.

Harrison Sheppard

INDEX

Made in the USA
Charleston, SC
31 July 2011